CHARLES DARWIN:
British
Naturalist

Mason Crest
450 Parkway Drive, Suite D
Broomall, PA 19008
www.masoncrest.com

Printed and bound in the United States of America.

First printing
9 8 7 6 5 4 3 2 1

Series ISBN: 978-1-4222-2839-5
ISBN: 978-1-4222-2844-9
ebook ISBN: 978-1-4222-8964-8

The Library of Congress has cataloged the
        hardcopy format(s) as follows:

Library of Congress Cataloging-in-Publication Data

Cook, Diane.
  Charles Darwin : British naturalist / Diane Cook.
      pages cm — (People of importance)
  Audience: Age 9.
  Audience: Grades 4 to 6.
  ISBN 978-1-4222-2844-9 (hardcover) — ISBN 978-1-4222-2839-5 (series) — ISBN 978-1-4222-8964-8 (ebook)
  1. Darwin, Charles, 1809-1882. 2. Naturalists—England—Biography—Juvenile literature. 3. Evolution (Biology)—Juvenile literature. I. Title.
  QH31.D2C66 2014
  576.8'2092—dc23
  [B]
                            2013006223

Produced by Vestal Creative Services.
www.vestalcreative.com
Illustrations copyright © 2000 Vitali P. Konstantinov.

People of Importance

CHARLES DARWIN:
British
Naturalist

Diane Cook   Vitali Konstantinov

Mason Crest

Where do people come from? This question has been answered in many different ways through the centuries. Ancient Chinese creation myths say that Nu-wa molded people out of clay. Two hundred years ago, most Europeans would have said, "God created people." Later, many came to believe people descended from apes.

For thousands of years, people wondered about the origin of human beings. In Europe, the church provided a reassuring answer—God created humans in his own image. The Bible says that God created all things in six days and he shaped Adam and Eve with his hands. Although some people questioned if this was a literal story, most people believed the Bible.

This was how things were when, in 1859, *On the Origin of the Species* appeared. It hit scientific and religious communities like a bombshell. Its scientific argument undermined the church's creation account, challenged old ideas and opened up a new field of scientific investigation.

DARWIN

Carcinus maenas

Gopherus polyphemus

Clemmys insculpta

Caiman Scleropsu

Hapalochlaena maculosa

Limulus moluccanus

Boa caninus

Eunectes murinus

Put simply, *On the Origin of Species* presents a theory of natural selection. It says that all living things came from a single ancestor, but over the generations and in the process of reproduction, many different species have evolved. However, not every evolved species survives. The natural resources of the planet are limited and there is not enough for everything, so those species that can best meet the demands and challenges of their environment will survive, while the others will slowly die out. Moreover, this is a process that is continuous and perpetual.

Charles Robert Darwin, an English scientist, is the author of this theory, which has significantly affected the way people think. You are probably thinking that a great man like Darwin was almost certainly a brilliant child, but he actually appeared to be rather ordinary. To be perfectly honest, some people may have even thought he was a bit dull. His primary school evaluations said he was an average student with average abilities. You see, Darwin often neglected his schoolwork in favour of more interesting things. His school principal even called him lazy. Had you known Darwin as a child, you too might have found it hard to imagine that he would one day grow up to do extraordinary things. So, how did this boy who showed little promise come to change the world?

Charles Robert Darwin was born in the spring of 1809. His father was a well-known doctor and his mother was the daughter of a rich and successful family. Charles grew up in comfort and was given the best education; however, he showed little interest in schoolwork and little ambition to achieve. Instead, he enjoyed walking through the woods and collecting things. He collected bird's eggs, mineral samples and insects. His room was full of specimens.

He liked to find out the names of plants. The amazing variety of living things fascinated him. Other people thought these activities were a waste of time. His father wanted him to become a doctor, a lawyer or someone of standing. His father scolded him once, saying, "You care for nothing but shooting, dogs and catching mice. You will disgrace yourself and your family."

Darwin knew his father was disappointed in him, but he really found his lessons very boring. The study of geography, history and Greek

did not bring him the excitement and happiness that the discoveries of nature offered. But to make his father happy, Darwin, who was 16 years old, joined his 18-year-old brother, studying medicine at Edinburgh University in Scotland.

Upon entering the university, Darwin discovered he had an unexpected freedom. Here, he could spend more time doing what he loved. He began to make friends with other people who shared his interests, and he joined naturalist societies. He collected specimens of ocean life and gave talks about

his observations and discoveries. Life was marvelous, except for his classes! He found anatomy and pharmacology even more uninteresting than Greek. But observing at the hospital was the worst. There was no anesthetic in those days, and patients had to bear the agony of surgery without painkillers. Darwin survived his first visit to the operating theatre, but he ran out during the second and refused to go back. The screams of the patients, the sight of their blood and the sound of their pain were too much to bear.

After this experience, Darwin decided he couldn't be a doctor and never again wanted to attend those classes.

∘ Dr. Robert Darwin ∘

Instead, he spent his days with his friends, discussing and investigating to his heart's content.

Of course, his father soon heard about this. "I hear you don't intend to become a doctor. Is that right?" he asked Darwin.

"No, I don't like it," Darwin replied. "Then, why not study to be a priest?" his father suggested.

Darwin figured that being a priest would give him lots of time to explore the countryside. He thought his father's suggestion was a smart one.

The next year, Darwin entered Cambridge University to study for the priesthood. His life there continued to

revolve around his other interests, but this time he paid more attention to his studies. No matter how much he disliked algebra, geometry and the classics, he made sure he passed them.

The most important thing Darwin got out of his time at Cambridge was a chance to associate with some scholarly people. Professor Henslow, a botanist who was to play a very important role in determining Darwin's future, was one of those. Henslow not only invited him to join scientific discussions, but also took him home for meals and out on field expeditions. Darwin's knowledge of biology increased greatly thanks to Henslow's influence. Henslow also introduced Darwin to other scholars. These scholars were all much older and were established in their fields, but they treated him like a friend.

After graduation, Darwin returned home. He had not been there for long when he received a most unexpected and exciting letter from Professor Henslow. It said, "The government is to send a ship to South America and the Pacific to conduct surveys. The captain would like to invite a young man to accompany them as an unpaid naturalist. This is a tremendous opportunity."

Darwin had never forgotten the book, *Wonders of the World*, that he'd borrowed as a child from one of his friends. He'd read it over and over, dreaming that one day he too would board a ship and sail around the world. Now he had a chance to make this dream come true! He immediately decided to accept.

Predictably, his father totally opposed Darwin's participation. "This will not help your career as a priest. Moreover, it is far too dangerous!" he said.

Darwin could think of no way of persuading his father, so he just looked at him, silently pleading with him to change his mind.

"I wanted you to become a doctor, but you wouldn't," his father said. "I wanted you to become a priest, but you aren't serious. You are a great disappointment to me." His father fell silent for a long time before finally saying, "If you can find any man of common sense who advises you to go, then I will give my consent."

Darwin immediately enlisted the aid of his most sympathetic supporter, his Uncle Jos. As expected, his uncle's reaction was the complete opposite of his father's.

"This is a most rare and wonderful opportunity! Let me go and persuade your father!" Without any hesitation, Jos climbed into his carriage and drove the 50-odd kilometres to Darwin's house to talk to his father.

The *Beagle* set sail for Devonport on 27 December, 1831. Darwin stood at the stern and watched as England slipped away. He felt a little apprehensive until he turned and looked at the wide expanse of ocean before him. Then his heart filled with curiosity and excitement as he wondered about what lay ahead.

After more than two months of sailing, the *Beagle* reached South America. The land was covered with virgin tropical forests and was home to countless insects, birds, animals and plants. Wherever the ship stopped, the crew immediately began surveying, and Darwin would start his explorations. Darwin, breathing the fresh air and

HMS BEAGLE

South America

rising with the sun, felt he was living the life of the angels.

Darwin found a rich diversity of animal life in South America. He wrote detailed observations in a diary and collected specimens, which he sent back to Professor Henslow. The problem with specimens was that they often deteriorated on the long trip back to England. Fortunately, less easily damaged specimens were also found—fossils. In a small village in Argentina, Darwin discovered the fossilised remains of some enormous animals and with a great deal of effort, had the whole pile moved onto the *Beagle*. The crew was less than impressed with this prize.

"This ship is small enough without having to fight for space with that pile of bones!" they complained, staring at the bone-covered deck.

The fossils were from large, extinct animals such as the giant sloth. The giant sloth looked very much like the sloth living today, except that it was so tall that it didn't need to climb trees to eat leaves. It could do so just sitting on the ground. There was also an animal called a toxodon that was as big as an elephant but had teeth like a mouse, and the eyes, ears and nostrils of an aquatic animal like the dugong.

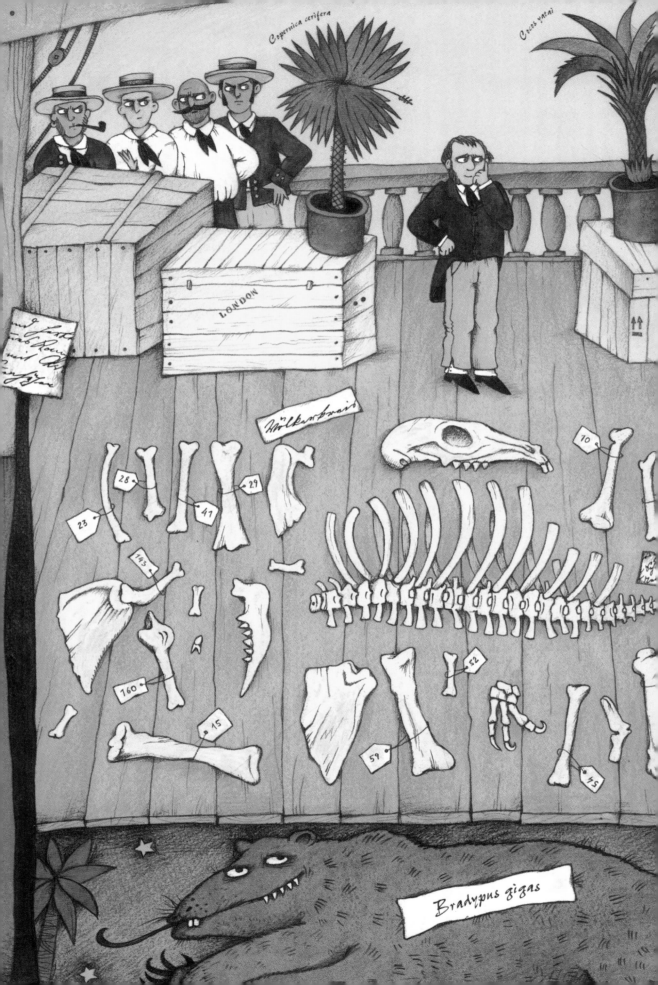

Darwin would sit on the deck examining these fossils and ask himself the same questions over and over: Why do characteristics belonging to distinctly different species today appear in these ancient extinct animals? Is it possible that several of today's species evolved from one ancestor? And why did these animals disappear from the earth? Are they related to the smaller animals of the same species living today and if so, how?

Having studied to be a priest, Darwin was very familiar with the Bible's solution to these questions. It said that long, long ago God decided to punish the world for its sins by sending a huge flood. Before the flood, Noah got two of all the animals alive today onto a boat and they were saved, but those that weren't on the boat, like the giant sloth, were drowned. Darwin also knew that geologists had shown the earth was millions of years old, while the church believed the world was only thousands of years old. The difference was too great. He began to doubt the church's interpretation of the Bible.

In 1835, the *Beagle* arrived in the Galapagos Islands. Galapagos means "giant tortoise," and true to the name, Darwin saw hundreds of huge tortoises crawling over all the islands. They were the local people's main food. One of the officials on the islands told Darwin with pride, "I can tell at a glance which island a tortoise was caught on, because the tortoises from each island look different. They even taste different."

This was extraordinary! The islands were close together, and they had similar climates and topography, yet the tortoises that lived on each of them were all different. How could that be? Was it possible that God had created different kinds of tortoises for each of the islands? No doubt there was a logical answer to all this, but all Darwin could see at the moment were the questions. The answers were still vague, shadowy

thoughts flickering in the back of his mind.

In 1836 the *Beagle* sailed back into Falmouth harbour. Darwin was delighted to see his own country again. He had left five years earlier, a 22-year-old youth, and was now returning a mature 27-year-old. His experiences on the journey poured out of him and he resolutely announced, "I thought about my future often during my five years away and decided I am not suited to being a priest. I have resolved to become a naturalist."

His father simply patted him on the shoulder and replied, "I don't need to worry about this boy anymore. He can manage his own life now."

Darwin began his new life in London. In 1839, he married his cousin Emma. He soon discovered that the detailed records he kept during his journey and the fossils he sent back to Henslow had created a great deal of interest in the scientific world. He, therefore, had plenty of opportunities to meet with noted scientists of the day to discuss and exchange ideas. London was an unpleasant place in which to live, but it was the only place where he could meet and work with such experts.

Everything was going well for Darwin. His marriage was loving and happy. The fossils he brought back were, with the help of other scientists, being analysed and categorised. He had also been made a fellow of the prestigious Royal Society. But then, unexpectedly, his health began to fail. He tired easily and had dizzy spells and palpitations. The slightest exertion was too much for him. Even talking to people made him ill. The doctors could not find the cause of his illness, and Darwin decided to leave dirty, smelly London and move to Down in the southeast of England to rest. It was clean and peaceful there, and since there were few visitors, Darwin once more had time to devote to his work.

Darwin had not forgotten the questions and ideas that had arisen during his time away from England. The origins of life constantly occupied his thoughts. How did all the many different species of plants and animals in this world come into being? The simple

Pan paniscus

Vulpes antarcticus

Pongo Pygmaeus

V.K

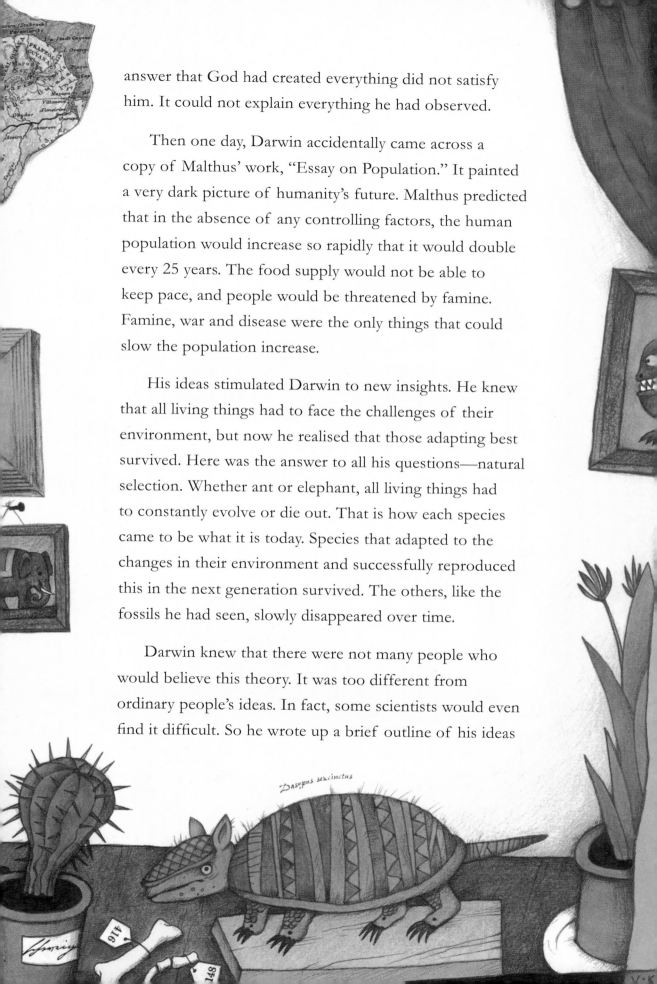

answer that God had created everything did not satisfy him. It could not explain everything he had observed.

Then one day, Darwin accidentally came across a copy of Malthus' work, "Essay on Population." It painted a very dark picture of humanity's future. Malthus predicted that in the absence of any controlling factors, the human population would increase so rapidly that it would double every 25 years. The food supply would not be able to keep pace, and people would be threatened by famine. Famine, war and disease were the only things that could slow the population increase.

His ideas stimulated Darwin to new insights. He knew that all living things had to face the challenges of their environment, but now he realised that those adapting best survived. Here was the answer to all his questions—natural selection. Whether ant or elephant, all living things had to constantly evolve or die out. That is how each species came to be what it is today. Species that adapted to the changes in their environment and successfully reproduced this in the next generation survived. The others, like the fossils he had seen, slowly disappeared over time.

Darwin knew that there were not many people who would believe this theory. It was too different from ordinary people's ideas. In fact, some scientists would even find it difficult. So he wrote up a brief outline of his ideas

Dasypus sexcinctus

and published them in a paper that naturalists received with interest, but no one knew he was working on a comprehensive theory of evolution.

Constantly troubled by ill health, Darwin worked quietly on his theory for more than 20 years. He spent his days researching and refining it but was never quite ready to publish. Only a few close friends knew what he was working on, and they constantly encouraged him to make

it public. But his theory was like a baby to him. He wanted it to be perfect and without defect.

Then in 1858 Darwin received a letter that shattered his peaceful existence. The letter was from Wallace, another naturalist. In it, he sent Darwin an essay on which he asked Darwin to comment. The essay contained the same ideas that Darwin had spent more than 20 years developing!

"Are they all wasted, then? All my years of hard work?" Darwin asked himself again and again. "Yet if I publish my work now, I will have betrayed Wallace's trust in me."

After much heart searching, Darwin decided to abandon his work but his friends wouldn't let him. "You can't throw away 20 years of work! You mustn't! There's got to be another way. Let us take care of it. We'll arrange it so that both you and Wallace can make your work public at the same time, but you've got to hurry up and write your book."

It took more than a year of hard work, but in 1859, Darwin's *On the Origin of Species* was finally published.

Darwin had worried that no one would buy his book, but the first edition of 1,250 copies was sold out on the first day, and a constant stream of people were ordering copies. It was obvious that people were full of curiosity about the origins of life. At the same time, and just as he had predicted, the book was greeted with waves of anger, fear and protest. Darwin was criticised by many scientists and denounced by the religious community who claimed his theory was blasphemous. They thought that if people had evolved from early forms of life, just as animals had, then humans would not still be God's beloved children, created in his own image. They did not understand that the Bible could be interpreted differently.

Articles and cartoons satirising Darwin appeared regularly in newspapers and magazines. The most common images were of Darwin's head on an ape's body or Darwin crawling among worms or other simple creatures. Darwin did nothing about these deliberate misrepresentations of his theory. He only smiled sadly. He had no wish

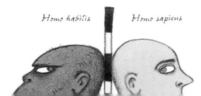

Homo habilis   Homo sapiens

Cardadvicus taiteri

CHARLES
ROBERT
DARWIN
·1809·1882

to new pasture
e larger quadr
but t

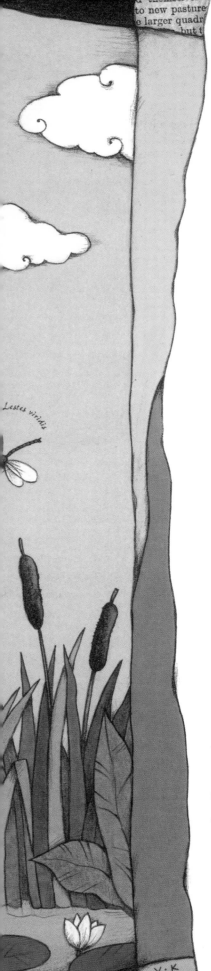

to waste time defending or explaining his ideas. Instead, he went on living his quiet, peaceful life, taking daily walks through the woods and continuing his scientific research and writing. Nevertheless, in his heart he hoped that one day people would understand that his purpose had not been to overturn God and destroy their beliefs, but just to prove one thing—that life was always changing.

Darwin died in 1892 in Down, as a result of a a heart problem. His wife and children originally wanted to bury him quietly in a small nearby church, but at the urging of scientists, publishers and society as a whole, they finally agreed to his being honoured with a grand funeral and burial in Westminster Abbey. By the time of his death, the scientific community had widely accepted the theory of evolution. Today it is believed by nearly all.

In the hundred years or so since Darwin's ideas first sparked research into the origins of life, great strides have been made in genetics and biology, giving people a much deeper understanding of the world. What we will never know, however, is what nature did one hundred years ago to cause a small boy who observed insects, birds and animals to devote his life and energies to finding answers to its mysteries. But if we are willing to go and look for ourselves, to explore the rich diversity of life around us, perhaps we too will find new questions to ask.

BIOGRAPHY

Author Diane Cook is a journalist and freelance writer. She has written hundreds of newspaper articles and writes regularly for national magazines, trade publications, and websites. She lives in Dover, Delaware, with her husband and three children.